Enneagram:

The Only Book You Will Ever Need to Build Strength for Your Life. Discover The 9 Personalities Types. Evolve Your Personality and Become Self Aware!

Table of Contents

Introduction......6

Chapter 1: The Enneagram and the Self......8

Chapter 2: The History of the Enneagram......19

Chapter 3: The Structure of the Enneagram......24

Chapter 4: The 9 Personality Types......30

Chapter 5: The Wings......94

Chapter 6: Health of the Self......99

Chapter 7: Personality Test......111

Conclusion......140

© Copyright 2018 by Ian Baron - All rights reserved.

The follow eBook is reproduced below with the goal of providing information that is as accurate and reliable as possible. Regardless, purchasing this eBook can be seen as consent to the fact that both the publisher and the author of this book are in no way experts on the topics discussed within and that any recommendations or suggestions that are made herein are for entertainment purposes only. Professionals should be consulted as needed prior to undertaking any of the action endorsed herein.

This declaration is deemed fair and valid by both the American Bar Association and the Committee of Publishers Association and is legally binding throughout the United States.

Furthermore, the transmission, duplication or reproduction of any of the following work including specific information will be considered an illegal act irrespective of if it is done electronically or in print. This extends to creating a secondary or tertiary copy of the work or a recorded copy and is only allowed with express written consent from the Publisher. All additional right reserved.

The information in the following pages is broadly considered to be a truthful and accurate account of facts and as such any inattention, use or misuse of the information in question by the reader will render any resulting actions solely under their purview. There are no scenarios in which the publisher or the original author of this work can be in any fashion deemed liable for any hardship or damages that may befall them after undertaking information described herein.

Additionally, the information in the following pages is intended only for informational purposes and should thus be thought of as universal. As befitting its nature, it is presented without assurance regarding its prolonged validity or interim quality. Trademarks that are mentioned are done without written consent and can in no way be considered an endorsement from the trademark holder.

Introduction

Congratulations on downloading *Enneagram* and thank you for doing so.

The following chapters will discuss several different aspects of what constitutes the Enneagram. Since the 1980's, the Enneagram has been used to evaluate someone's personality and reveal the true self. Its true origin reaches much further back beyond that, and as time has passed, the Enneagram has had many different people try to alter its interpretation. This has created some confusion. This book aims to clear up the mystifications that have been surrounding the Enneagram for far too long.

There are several different aspects to the Enneagram that are often overlooked. The Wings and integration/disintegration points are only some of the very important pieces of the Enneagram that do not get covered often. Without being familiar with the entire Enneagram, there will always be confusion surrounding it. In this book, just about every single piece of the Enneagram will be covered. From the 9 different types of dominant personalities, all the way down to how they interact with each other, the mysteries of the Enneagram will be unveiled to you. There will also be a personality test to help you along the path of self-discovery. If you have been wondering who you are, who you *really* are, then the Enneagram is here to help answer that question.

There are plenty of books on this subject on the market, thanks again for choosing this one! Every effort was made to ensure it is full of as much useful information as possible, please enjoy!

Chapter 1: The Enneagram and the Self

Do you know yourself? Are you sure? Can you really explain the reasons for every action you have ever performed? Do you really know the root causes that underline every emotion you have ever felt? Are you capable of understanding the inspiration that has preceded every thought that has ever formulated inside your mind? Unless you have already braved the opaque waters of self-reflection, the answers to these questions should be a strong and resounding NO!

Since the birth of humanity, most people have simply acted or reacted, without delving into the motivations that dictate their actions. This is because we are human beings, far from perfect but high above all the other creatures that we share the planet earth with. Since humans are the highest and most complex out of all the intelligence on earth, it comes with the territory that our thoughts, emotions, and actions are infinitely more complicated than every other living creature. This, upon the first realization, can seem like a bad luck of the draw or being dealt an unfair card from the deck of life. Just by being born as humans, we are confounded into an existence that is more confusing and complicated to navigate through than every other creature on earth.

    Compare the life of a human to the life of a deer. A deer, lower in the scale of mental/emotional development and somatic functions than a person, does not have anywhere near the amount of variability to sift through as does a human being. When a deer is scared, it runs away. When it is hungry or thirsty, it fills its stomach. During mating season, it looks for a mate. When it is tired, it sleeps. When it has found its herd, it romps and travels with them. Instinct pervades every decision a deer makes and gives it an existence that is closer to automatic than cognitive. This – comparing a deer to a human – may seem course, because it is. Among creatures lower in scale than humans, there certainly is variability in what they do and in the types of personalities they display, but even so, they still do not have to ponder the great questions that many of us ask ourselves all too often; "Who am I?" "Why did I do that?" "What was I thinking at that moment?"

Animals, insects, plants, and microbes do not have to waddle through the muddy waters of self-discovery. Their existences are simple, automatic, and one could even argue, destined to fate. Even if a creature lower than a human was to act out of character, they would not question why they did so. Nor can they even conceptualize the idea of self-improvement and prevent their negative traits from manifesting again. They simply live to live until they die and then nature creates another one to fill in the gap that they have left behind after expiring. That may sound harsh, but self-discovery is concerned with the truth, and the truth can hurt equally as much as it can heal.

On the other hand, humans are constantly berated with new experiences, environments, and stimuli. Compared to a deer, our lives are far from simple and automatic – or at least they should be. Every single day we have to make judgment calls and perform actions that can have consequences that extend far past the current moment. This applies to even the most common and mundane of our activities. Like a deer, we get hungry and sleepy, but we can decide what to eat and how much of it. We can decide when to go to sleep and set alarms to tell us that it's time to wake up. We can even bypass meals and sleep or change our diets along with sleeping arrangements. These examples of hunger and sleep are extremely baseline. Now, just push the idea a little further. Remember back to a recent business meeting, social gathering or a date that you went on. How many thoughts did you have during those interactions? How many different feelings passed through you? What actions did you perform, or choose not to perform? Surely you encountered a wider range of sensations than a deer does in its daily life. Upon the first realization of the consequences that are attached to our natural mental/emotional superiority over lower lifeforms, it really can seem like us humans have drawn the short end of the stick. We are forced to decipher more options and overcome more challenges than everything else. We have to manage a wider range of cognitive functions, both positive and negative, than all the other beasts of the world.

Without question, humans have the most complicated lives on the planet. However, we have something to compensate for this seemingly apparent disadvantage. Human beings can self-reflect. Unlike an animal, we can probe into our psyches and better learn who we really are, and thus, understand why we do the things we do, feel the things we feel, and think the thoughts we think. We can use our powers of associative learning and self-discipline to better understand our own motivations and behavioral patterns. We can do what an animal cannot, which is learning about ourselves. After that, we can begin to (through hard work and allotting time) start to enhance which aspects of ourselves that we find beneficial and remove the aspects that stunt us from reaching a higher potential. We have not drawn the shorter stick in nature; it only appears that way at first glance.

Even so, to fully utilize our latent abilities and direct how our individual growth develops, we require tools (another advantage we have over other creatures). Among the many different cognitive tools that exist there is one known as the Enneagram which has been designed to do directly aid in the process of self-reflection.

Consider the Enneagram to be a simplified schematic of the human psyche. Now, keep in mind that even though the Enneagram may be simplified, the human psyche is the most complicated concept that we know of. Modern science still struggles to define what consciousness actually is and what it is not. In many ways, the questions of "Who am I" or "Why did I do that?" are the forerunners to the bigger mysteries of existence. Figuring out the answers to those questions is the first step to understanding your own consciousness, and thus, understanding who you really are. The Enneagram can be used as a sort of roadmap to help clear the road of your consciousness and show the way to who you really are, instead of wandering through life like a clueless animal that is completely at the mercy of its environment.

To understand the Enneagram is not the easiest task upon first discovery but, with time and practice, it will help clear the waters of confusion that surround yourself and others around you. The more you learn about it, the clearer its implications will become and help to shed light on the questions of why you, or someone else, may think or act in a certain way.

The Enneagram can be broken-down into one little symbol. It consists of the numbers 1-9 and intersecting lines between each number. When someone first sees the Enneagram, they may write it off as just some confusing chart, a mess that lacks cohesion. This is the first error that many people make when first trying to swim across the channel from ignorance to self-discovery. Every number and line encased within the Enneagram contains a wealth of specifics meanings. Nothing in the image is arbitrary or random. It just has to be learned how to be read, then it can be studied, and then you can use the emblem of the Enneagram to discover who you really are, as well as see the truths of other people. The Enneagram will unbiasedly reveal your own strengths, virtues, limitations, and vices. The Enneagram will tell you what you need to improve about yourself. It will help you to discover which traits of the self should be removed if you desire to grow into a more efficient version of who you already are. It will aid you in the process of no longer living like an automatic animal and graduating into a completely self-sufficient human being. It will give you the set of keys that can unlock the doors to your life that have always been shut tight. It will help you to truly know yourself on every level.

The first thing most people will notice when seeing the Enneagram are the numbers 1-9. These 9 numbers are all representative of the different types of personality a person can have. Each one of these personality types should not be summed up into only one or two sentences. Yes, that can be done, and in many different mediums related to the Enneagram, it has been. Yet, the enneagram is used to learn everything you can about your own personality. Not superficially, but in depth. Remember that the enneagram is a schematic of the human psyche and that humans have the most complex psyches on the planet. One-word descriptions for something so complicated lacks both scope and substance.

To fully understand the Enneagram, and understand everything about you, every point of interest involved in the symbol must be taken into consideration. The major points of interest when studying the enneagram are:

- The 9 different personality types.
- The wings (secondary personality traits).
- The 9 levels of development of the personality.

- Integration and disintegration points.

Every piece of the Enneagram will be covered in this book – every number, line, shape, and all the points of interest listed above. But before delving into all of that, it would be wise to learn a little bit of the history that helped construct the enneagram. You are welcome to skip ahead and go straight to studying the enneagram if you wish but doing so is not recommended. Consider the history of the Enneagram a primer for what is to come. Many people have begun their research into the Enneagram expecting a short and insightful cognitive spell only to realize that it is a symbol that can be studied for an entire lifetime, and even then, there is still more to learn about it. You are never done discovering who you really are. You do have to start somewhere though, and the Enneagram is one of the best places to begin your journey of self-discovery.

Chapter 2: The History of the Enneagram

Covering every aspect of what has developed the Enneagram of personality would consist of not only just one book but an entire chronicling of all human thought. That may sound like a lofty statement, but it surely is not. The origin of the Enneagram can be traced back to the days of antiquity. In truth, it is an expansion of spiritual and early psychological concepts that have been streamlined to be understood by a larger and more contemporary audience. Esoteric concepts such as the "Law of Three" or "Law of Seven" are concluded in some circles to be directly connected to the development of the Enneagram. The work of Eliphas Levi, Helena Blavatsky, Pythagoras, among many others who are renown in the realm of esoteric workings, have all been attributed to having at least some input with constructing the modern-day version of the

Enneagram (or using their own versions of the symbol). It is recommended to, eventually, study some of the theories that the previously named people developed, but that is for a later time along with your journey of self-exploration.

The currently used model of the Enneagram is accredited to being discovered (or altered) by Oscar Ichazo. He was not the first person to show the Enneagram to the world at large, but he was the one who attributed the 9 basic personality types to the image, which is what the Enneagram is most famously known for in our current era. Oscar Ichazo was the man who took the Enneagram of antiquity and shaped it into the Enneagram of personality, as it is known today. Even though the Enneagram has origins that trace back much further, Ichazo's interpretation of the symbol only goes back to the 1960's.

Oscar Ichazo was a very well learned man who traveled abroad. He was born in Bolivia, moved to Peru, and then relocated to Argentina. Later in life, he traveled to different parts of South America and Asia where he learned a large variety of different spiritual and psychological theories and techniques. This all led up to him establishing the Arica school in Chile. At this school, he focused his teachings on understanding and expanding the human consciousness. It was believed back in the era of antiquity, and still by many people today that grasping the truth of the self and the nature of existence as a whole can only be accurately understood by first understanding your own consciousness. Although Ichazo used many different tools and symbols to explore the human consciousness, the Enneagram of personality (with the 9 basic personality types he attributed to it) became one of the main instruments he often employed.

While Oscar Ichazo was teaching his lessons at the school of Arica, he also taught two American writers and psychologists, John Lilly and Claudio Naranjo. Claudio Naranjo, later on, began spreading his own particular interpretations of the Enneagram in America during the 1970s. Since then, many other authors, psychologists, and spiritual leaders have spread their own version and lessons of the Enneagram. This has created a double-edged sword of confusion and debate to its practical use and applications. In truth, the Enneagram can be extrapolated to represent many different things, but its focus has always been concentrated on development and understanding of the self.

The theories and uses of the Enneagram differ among those who attest to it, as some attribute it more to the soul while others like to remove spiritual implications from it. Whether your particular journey of self-realization is imbued with spiritual essence, or if you select to omit spirituality from studying the Enneagram, it can be used the same way. Begin learning about it with the mindset that you are most comfortable with. As you learn more about the Enneagram, and yourself, be aware that your goals and current concepts of understanding may change quite drastically.

Chapter 3: The Structure of the Enneagram

Oscar Ichazo specifically used the Enneagram to dissect and explore different aspects of the human soul. He placed a special importance on how the different essences of a person may become distorted or fall into unbeneficial states of ego. Drawing inspiration from many different schools of spiritual and psychological thought, including the Tree of Life, Ichazo established a wide variety of correspondences to each of the 9 dominant personality types. These included:

- The major characteristic of the dominant personality type.
- What the ego could negatively fixate its attention towards, operating within the sphere of a specific personality type.
- A frame of mind associated with a dominant personality type when it was

exalted (sometimes called a "Holy Idea").

- Baseline desires and fears that were attached to a dominant personality type. Along with these were also the attributed vices and virtues.
- Certain temptations that were harder for a dominant personality type to resist.
- Integration and disintegration points for each type of personality. These are also known as "growth" and "stress" points. For now, think of these as how someone's personality can alter when they are in good or bad moods.

As more people started adding and subtracting their own correspondences to the Enneagram, much of the spiritual aspects have been lessened. The basic model of the Enneagram has not changed in a long time though, and no matter how you decide to study the symbol, the schematic remains the same. The quickest way to make sense of the

Enneagram is to personally draw one. Grab a pen and a piece of paper and follow these directions.

- First, draw a circle. A circle is a symbol of unity, wholeness, and nothing being separate from each other. Consider the circle as a sphere of operation. Whatever exists outside the circle has no effect on what takes place within the circle. Whatever exists within the circle is connected to everything else within the sphere of operation.

- Label the numbers 1-9 around the perimeter of the circle. Start with 9 at the top, then going clockwise, list the numbers 1-8. When you are done, the number 9 should be sandwiched between the number 1 (to its right) and the number 8 (to its left). These numbers are the 9 basic dominant personality types.

- Draw a triangle between the numbers 9, 6, and 3. Consider the triangle to be symbolic of something coming into being, the first possible shape.
- Draw a line connecting to each number in the following order; 1-4-2-8-5-7-1. Drawing a connecting line to these numbers will create an irregular hexagram. Think of the irregular hexagram as a representation of abstraction being brought into form.

- Outside of the circle, write the following words next to each number. 9 – Mediator. 1 – Perfectionist. 2 – Helper. 3 – Achiever. 4 – Individualist. 5 – Investigator. 6 – Loyalist. 7 – Enthusiast. 8 – Challenger.

Congratulations! You have just drawn the Enneagram of personality. Between the images used in this book and the picture you have just drawn, you can begin to use the Enneagram to explore yourself. These few building blocks of a circle, triangle, irregular hexagram, intersecting lines, and the numbers 1-9 may not seem like much at first, but when you learn what they all mean, illumination will begin to be unfurled to you.

The words you wrote next to the numbers 1-9 are the names of the different dominant personality types. According to different sources, some of these personality types have different names. Do not get stuck on the minute details of the Enneagram and remember that one-word descriptions of the 9 different dominant personality types are only a starting point - not the finish line of understanding. As you discover more about it and become capable of drawing your own conclusions, you may alter names and associations as you see fit.

Now that you have been introduced to the Enneagram and know some of the histories that have helped develop it, you can safely begin to study each personality type individually and begin to discover the aspects of yourself that you didn't know about before.

Chapter 4: The 9 Personality Types

To fully understand everything that makes up someone's personality, the entire sphere of the Enneagram must be taken into consideration. The 9 basic personality types are only the start of studying the Enneagram and yourself. It should always be remembered though that every person has a dominant personality – which will be one of the basic 9 types listed in this chapter. It should also be made clear that your dominant personality will not always be acting with precedence over other aspects of your personality. Your secondary traits, as well as other factors, will have an effect on how you are thinking or behaving at any given moment. In truth, every person has all of the basic 9 personality types inside their psychosis. However, no matter what stimulus alters our personality temporarily, you will always return to your basic personality type. This is why the basic personality types are labeled as the *Dominant Personality*. Before diving into the secondary personality traits, as well as all the other extrapolated pieces of the human personality, it's best to learn what the 9 dominant personality types are. We start at the top and work our way down the tree of the Enneagram.

Although behavioral science is still developing, it is understood that we develop a dominant personality early in life. Hereditary factors, family traditions, environment, social, and early childhood experiences all come together to create a dominant personality that we clothe ourselves in. Think of your dominant personality as a persona that you wear to navigate and understand the world around you. It can change, for better or worse, as time goes by, but no matter how your personality alters, it will always have roots stemming from the dominant personality that you developed during the first four or five years of your life.

You are the soil. The dominant personality is the first root to spring from the soil, and everything else that develops after are the fruit that hangs from the tree of your personality. The tree of your personality can either thrive with time or wither. Using a tool like the Enneagram will help you to make it thrive.

Along with describing what each of the 9 dominant personality types is, there will be a list of the metadata that goes along with each one. These will include the virtues, vices, desires, fears, what the ego can fixate on, exalted ideals, temptations, and integration and disintegration points. The integration and disintegration points will be explained more in detail later, but a cursory explanation should be given here.

When someone, let's use a person with a type 1 dominant personality as an example, is having a bad week, they will not act like themselves, so to speak. They will move away from the normal dominant personality and "fall" into a different type of person. This is known as disintegrating. When a person with a type 1 dominant personality "falls" into a slump, they will disintegrate into a type 4. Whenever they pull out of this slump and return to their normal selves, they will readopt the persona of a type 1. On the other end of the spectrum, when they are having a good week, they will integrate into a Type 7. Then when their good luck streak winds down, they will return to Type 1. Be aware at all times that there is no superiority in relation to the numbers assigned to each type of personality. Just because someone is a 1 or a 4 does not mean they are better off than someone with a different number. The numbers are used for organizational purposes only. Later on, when the integration/disintegration points are covered in more detail, this will all become clearer. For now, just be aware that when someone is in a slump or on a winning streak, their personality will change temporarily.

It should also be understood that none of the 9 basic personality types are exclusive to either gender. Although they may be expressed in different manners, both men and women have all of the basic 9 personality types within their psyches. Your gender will only affect the way that your dominant personality presents itself, not what your dominant personality actually is. Also, remember that any of these 9 dominant personality types can all manifest in different ways and that each one is working in tandem with secondary personality traits as well as other factors incorporated in the human psyche. In other words, although your dominant personality type may be a 3, on some days, you may act more like a 4 or 7. Recognizing these sorts of fluctuations in your behavioral pattern is just another part along the road to self-discovery.

Type 1: The Perfectionist and Reformer

Type 1 people are the kind of people that feel they must be correct with everything they do. They believe themselves to adhere to a higher moral code than other people. They place strong values on being recognized for their integrity and having a higher standard of principles. They are typically very disciplined people and are not the easiest to sway away from their goals. Structure and order are important concepts to Type 1s as they tend to want the world around them to be as disciplined as they are. Type 1s are the kind of people that you can rely on to uphold the rules and follow procedures down to the letter. These are the kind of people that you can trust to get a job done well the first time you ask, and they can probably do it without asking for help. Most Type 1s do not only mind hard work but thrive while doing it. However, if their work environment is not as perfect as they are, then they may have trouble trying to complete a task. Due to this, some Type 1s can be slow to move from the planning stage into action. They can be procrastinators, or not even begin some projects at all if they don't see the immediate value in doing so. They can be somewhat slow at times to make decisions while they meticulously comb through all the variables of every decision they make.

Type 1s make good leaders, although those they are leading may think they are too strict or rigid. They are also very talented at noticing all the finer details and catching the little things that others would often miss. They can organize and turn a wild incoherent mess into something where all the pieces fit together. They can shape chaos into order.

Due to their need to feel perfect, they can be susceptible to harsh judgment towards themselves and others. When a Type 1 discovers that they have made a mistake, they take it more harshly than others would. They can also hold every single little thing, including other people, up to their standards – which can come across as very unfair and unrealistic. They can be prone to self-doubt and question every action they make. A common Type 1 will often ask themselves if they are good enough to accomplish whatever they are trying to do and often second guess things that they had already done.

Type 1s do not have much patience towards the irresponsible. They are prone to bursts of anger but often will try to hide it from others. Being angry can be a sign of not being perfect, which is all they aspire to be. When trying to hide their anger, they may display subtle body language to reflect their anger or just go as silent as a stone. They may even start to become extremely formal and overtly polite as a way of masking the imperfection of anger. If they do become angry enough to seek some sort of vengeance, they will most likely extract it with a cold and calculating methodology. They like to plan ahead, and even their schemes of revenge must be executed perfectly. An easy way to get on the bad side of a Type 1 and arouse their anger is to point out their imperfections and be as critical of them as they are of others. A Type 1 is already judging themselves on a regular basis, and when someone else starts doing it to them as well, they simply don't want to hear it, especially since the person who is criticizing them is already imperfect in their eyes.

Type 1s can be hard to argue with. They already believe themselves to be correct and may completely detach themselves from the present moment. Or they may get all too caught up in it. It depends on if they think the other people around them are worthy of bothering over.

Type 1s are also the reformers. They fix errors and strive to set everything in its proper place. Spiritually speaking, they seek the highest platitude. They will endure whatever challenge they must so they can learn, grow, and ascend onto higher plains. There can even be a sacrificial aspect to Type 1s. If they understand that there is something they must do, or stop doing, to achieve a higher grade of consciousness, then a Type 1 will readily meet the challenge head-on. Type 1s can become dogmatic and may misinterpret or discard concepts that do not fit into their dogma. It can take a lot of time for them to learn their lessons. Yet, when they do learn them, they go straight to work trying to reform their errors.

Type 1 at a glance

- **Virtue:** Being serene. Feeling as if there are no other improvements needed.
- **Vice:** Prone to anger when feeling that everything is not as it should be.
- **Common Temptation:** Criticizing others and themselves.

- **Common Desire:** Being recognized as being correct. Being in balance.
- **Common Fear:** Being wrong or swayed by other people. Being out of balance.
- **Exalted Ideals:** Being correct in their principles. Serving a worthy purpose. Correcting errors of the self and their environment.
- **Egoic Challenge:** Type 1s have to try very hard not to hold resentment against everything that does not fall in line with what they consider to be perfection. They need to let go of the desire to judge and control everything around them.
- **Integration Point:** 7.
- **Disintegration Point:** 4

Type 2: The Helper and Giver

Type 2s aim to develop strong relationships with others. They will often go out of their way to win over another person. These types of people are the helping hands, the people you can call upon when stuck in a jam. They feel a sense of satisfaction when they know they have helped someone. Generally, they also like to receive recognition for their efforts and are more likely to assist someone they know who can spread a good word of their reputation, but they may also feel a sudden impulse to help out a stranger as well. The major motivation behind their actions is a longing to feel apricated, even needed, by other people. This is not vanity, as Type 2s are also humble people. A type 2 depends upon the opinions of others to give value to themselves. This can parlay into random acts of kindness and generosity. They can also influence others with their kindness and spread it around infectiously. To a Type 2, doing so is a roundabout way of making the world a better place to live.

Every type of dominant personality has positive and negative traits. Type 2s sound almost perfect, but it should be known that they can lack confidence if they are not receiving praise from others. They don't just want to help; they need to help someone to feel as if they are worthy human beings. Type 2s want people to depend on them. There could be a deeper confliction hidden here, as if a Type 2 may not feel that they deserve love or affection for who they are and must earn it by helping other people. Some Type 2s can come across as manipulative. They help someone fully expecting the help to be returned to them and are not offering assistance for free even if they pretend they are. They will often give out many compliments but expect other people to do the same to them.

Type 2s are crowd-pleasers. They are the sort of people who will show up to a party with gifts or buy everyone at the bar an extra round. Most people are attracted to them since they can come off as warm and comforting. They don't mind giving up some of their time or resources if it means that other people will recognize them for their efforts. A Type 2 may not ask for anything in return for all that they give – but they still expect their good deeds to be rewarded in one manner or another.

Type 2s can be empathetic. They can notice when someone else is having a problem and will leap right into action to fix whatever is wrong. Because of their giving nature, they can become offended when ignored or their efforts are not recognized. They detest being taken advantage of, but still may let it happen anyway.

All the giving and helping that a Type 2 does is really a tactic to establish good relationships with people. Deep relationships are extremely important to them. Their generosity is on open display and acts like a net to catch the attention and goodwill of others.

They also try to resist negative stimulus and want everyone else around them to act as generous as they do. They can give advice without even being asked and are very quick to defend someone that they think has been wronged.

Since Type 2s are empaths, they can notice problems and desires that other people don't even notice about themselves. This can backfire on them though as they can spend too much time and effort on others and not themselves. They can also be susceptible to inflated egos if they are praised too much, and most of their social circle depends upon them to help all the time. Still, they are naturally humble people and have their boosted egos deflated if they fail to correctly help someone. They can also worry about other people when it is not necessary. One of the more detrimental things about a Type 2 is that they may lack the ability to do things alone. They need someone else to tell them that they did well. They can also become attention seekers.

They can become so wrapped up in other people that they can miss many things about themselves. They often don't realize that the reason they are helping others is due to wanting something in return for all the assistance they give. They can also force themselves onto people, and then lose interest in them quite quickly. Conflicts of interest may arise in their lives if they are trying to help more than one person and have to pick and choose who deserves it more. This can also scatter their focus and use of energy and fail to recognize that different people have different needs and desires, or attitudes and values. A Type 2 may try to help someone who doesn't need it and just get in the way. Or they may assume what someone's values are and become crushed when they learn that the person they are trying to help does not view the world the same way they do. Since they desire intimacy and deep connections so much, other people may just think of them as clingy.

They can subconsciously express their own needs onto others without realizing it. This indirect way of communicating can create rifts and delays in achieving their goals. They can also make the mistake of thinking everyone else is in need, even if the people they are trying to help are doing just fine. They can mistake this as being taken for granted. A Type 2 may dislike someone, but still jump in to help them anyway since they think that will increase the bond. They can brag about how helpful they are and have a fear of being rejected. They really just want to be loved and are doing everything they can to attract love towards them.

When Type 2ss are in their highest aspect, they won't expect anything in return. They give just to give and giving is its own reward. An exalted Type 2 will keep a positive mindset and believe that, even if they are not around to help, someone else will step in and fill their role. They will also understand that to better help others, they must be able to take care of themselves first. They understand that along with spreading love around, self-love is equally as important.

Spiritually, there is a sense of sacrifice here as well, but not the same that is associated with Type 1s. A Type 1 will sacrifice what they need to so they can become better for themselves, to raise their consciousness to higher planes. A Type 2 will sacrifice for the good of others and try to lift other people up to higher spiritual arenas with them.

Type 2 at a glance

- **Virtue:** Being Humble. They are prone to humility and can induce it without much effort.

- **Vice:** Too much pride. They can fall into a belief that they are the source of another person's happiness.
- **Common Temptation:** Manipulating other people with their kindness, including themselves and ignoring their own needs.
- **Common Desire:** Love.
- **Common Fear:** Not being loved, despite all they do.
- **Exalted Ideals:** Being free. If everyone is helping out each other, then there should be no more hurdles left to overcome.
- **Egoic Challenge:** Extreme flattery. They can become fixated on wanting other people to tell them how great they are.
- **Integration Point:** 4
- **Disintegration Point:** 8

Type 3: The Achiever and Performer

Type 3s are very concerned with image. They prefer to have the world around them notice that they are the very best at whatever they set themselves to. They often excel in whatever field of work they decide to enter. They are adaptable and efficient. These are some of the hardest working people out there and are often recognized as being pillars of the workplace. Types 3s often reached their goals and do so with gusto. Type 3s on the higher end of the spectrum serves as an inspiration to others. On the lower end, they can be dismissive and selfish. Type 3s place a larger emphasis on what they are doing, not on who they are outside of trying to reach their goals. Almost everything involved in the life of a Type 3 revolves around the idea of winning and losing.

They have a high drive for success and are very ambitious. Nothing matters as much to a Type 3 as results. How they get the results is another matter. Expect high levels of energy to surround type 3s as they are go-getters. They can alter their persona to match whatever task needs to be completed. They are capable of altering many different aspects of themselves. They can wear different guises and impress a large array of people. Some of them are not above lying or bending the rules a bit to stack things in their favor. Still, other Type 3s hold honesty as a high esteem and will place the concept on a pedestal.

They can be fiercely competitive even when there is no worthwhile reward to gain for their efforts. This can turn away many of the people they are trying to impress. They often seek out forms of competition even in their recreational activities, alone or on a team. They are also selective about whom they socialize with. They like to be on the winning team. This can make them good leaders, if even for the wrong reasons.

When a 3 makes a mistake, they are more likely to look at it as a learning experience than a failure. They can be closed minded though and overlook something that they don't understand - thinking that it is not worth their precious time. They think fast on their feet, and this can sometimes lead them to miss the little things, never stopping to smell the roses or appreciate someone else's good values. Also, when a 3 does not have a goal to reach, they can become wayward and start attaching value to missions that are not important. They can make a mountain out of an anthill. They can suffer from confusion of identity since they place so much value on work and accomplishments. They think they are their job, instead of realizing that their job is just an extension of who they really are. Type 3s can also misunderstand that their constant drive for winning is actually born of the need to compare themselves to other people. Type 3s can be thrown off-kilter when discovering that someone else may not care about all their worldly accomplishments. They can become self-conscious, and not in a good way.

They are capable of separating their emotions from their actions since emotions can get in the way of winning. They are not the best when it comes to deeper genuflection. They can also pretend to ignore feelings of despair and anxiety, even if these are traits that they should work through to become more successful. By ignoring sadness, they instead exude negativity in the form of anger. They also waver in front of authority and can become brown noses or try far too hard to impress someone up to the point where they come across as a nuisance. They do not take many risks, preferring to stay on the side of safety and success.

Despite the drive of a Type 3, their self-conscious nature places the most value on how other people perceive them. They are aiming for success not so much to better themselves, but to impress other people. Externally, they are very optimistic, but there is a strong fear of failure boiling inside their hearts. Masking their true feeling and fears can eventually create a web of stress that can plague their minds and distract them from truly opening up. Short outbursts and change of character are not uncommon in them. They may be winners, but unless someone else is announcing their victories, they will feel like losers.

When a 3 is discovered lying or not being who they really are, they can become defensive and spiteful. They may also spend too much time trying to impress the wrong people when what they should be doing is calming down and smelling the roses. Their confusions of identity are often noticed by other people before they notice it themselves. They are very good at doing what they set their minds to and adapting, but not so good at entering unfamiliar territory where the advantage is not stacked in their favor. They can also become delusional when they start to believe their own hype too much.

They can be emotionally closed off and are not willing to sustain a difficult heart to heart conversation. This can make their romantic lives a blithering mess. Often, a Type 3 will want a partner that is subservient to their aspirations. They also may not take criticism very well and can be labeled as coldhearted, even if it is not true. They may blame other people for making them look bad even if it is their own fault and can be very impatient. They need to feel validated at all times. Despite all their negative traits, they usually do well and are self-sufficient. They must keep in mind though, that their own arrogance can limit them from growing, and become the cause of their downfall.

Type 3 at a glance

- **Virtue:** Being authentic. When a Type 3 is at peace, they will see no reason to be dishonest or bend to rules. They think themselves to be winners without the need to cheat.
- **Vice:** Deceit and trickery. When not winning, a Type 3 will bend their own moral code to get back on track to victory, despite what they may have to do to get there.
- **Common Temptation:** Being better than others. Bragging and trying too hard is common with Type 3's.
- **Common Desire:** Giving value to whatever enterprise they are involved in.
- **Common Fear:** Not having value. They often worry about being worthless or replaceable.
- **Exalted Ideals:** Hope. Even when down, a Type 3 does not give up easily.

Where there is a will, there is a way. They truly believe that the effort they put in will return to them.
- **Egoic Challenge:** Conceit. It can be very difficult for a Type 3 to humble themselves. If another person humbles them, it can be crushing.
- **Integration Point:** 6
- **Disintegration Point:** 9

Type 4: The Individualist and Romantic

Type 4s have a longing desire to be noticed as being one of a kind. They are known as romantics due to their sensitivity. If something in their life lacks meaning, they will find a way to give it meaning. These sorts of people are not afraid to probe themselves and look for deeper significance throughout their days. Many people with a Type 4 personality make great artists and inventors. They do not chase after other people, preferring to give off an air of mystery and have others chase them. When someone does make an effort to know them, they often appreciate the sentiment. They may, however, try to pass their emotions onto others as a tactic to invoke compassion from people.

Type 4s feel a need to express how unique they are. Being individuals and not being lobbed into groups is important to them. When a Type 4 is operating on a higher polarity, they are content, even if they remain sensitive. They are acutely aware of what their emotions are and will probe deeper if need be. Diving into the darker side of the self can take great amounts of courage, and even if it is not always on display, Type 4s are willing to explore sides of themselves that others often avoid. They are also very good at finding the missing pieces and can solve many riddles and puzzles. The creativity of Type 4s knows almost no boundary. These combinations of characteristics can create a person that is very driven and can be an inspiration to others.

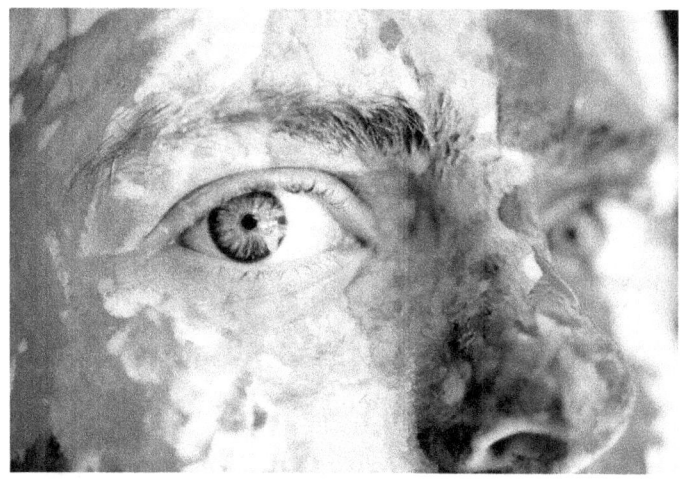

Feelings are always at the front of a Type 4's mind. They can pick up on the subtle hints of themselves, others, and the environment. They may even be able to pick out emotions in people before the other person notices it themselves. Not a single area in the spectrum of emotions is alien to a Type 4. This can have a negative side effect though. They can come across to others as temperamental and can be victims of mood swings. Switching from extreme joy to extreme sadness within minutes can happen to type 4s and keep them out of balance. They tend to take life a bit too seriously and may have trouble lightening up.

They seek out people that they can share the depths of their thought and feelings with. This can create long-lasting bonds, or they may come across as annoying to others. Since a 4 is usually looking for deeper meaning, they do not excel at small talk. They can exaggerate many of their own stories and place the emphasis of most conversations on themselves.

Typically, a 4 will feel that something is missing in their life. This can cause them to easily become envious of other people. They also may harp on the negative too much and beat themselves up for no good reason. They may have a plethora of amazing qualities about themselves but ignore them, and instead focus on what is wrong. They also have trouble separating emotions from other aspects of life and can become very bias, even bigotry. They place more trust in their own experiences and may not take advice or criticism well. A Type 4 needs to go to great lengths to keep up their esteem, and they often get easily bored with mundane routines. All in all, a Type 4 is looking to be understood and accepted.

More often than not, other types of people will feel pushed away by 4s. Their unique natures and need to create deep bonds can repel people away, as Type 4s may not come across as fun or easygoing. Some people may consider them to be downers, always focusing on what is missing in life. They are often labeled as bad listeners, even though they are usually very good at listening. They require more time to express themselves, and this can cause them to get left behind or feel as if they were. They do not like to be interrupted while expressing themselves.

They may want to continue pursuing something after it has already finished, beating a dead horse. Type 4s have also been labeled as drama queens or being melodramatic. Yet, when a Type 4 places all their emotional energy into some form of art, they often can stir the emotions of other people as deeply as their own water of emotion is raging in themselves.

In the end, a Type 4 wants to learn everything they can about themselves. They are self-explorers. This makes them naturals when it comes to spiritual pursuits. They are willing to go both into the dark and the light. They are natural loners but do not want to be. For Type 4s who are aiming for spiritual ascension, they can often find the companionship they are looking for in search of the divine.

Type 4 at a glance

- **Virtue:** Balancing their emotions. When a Type 4 is operating at their best, they can steady the violent waters and maintain peace through emotional adversity and confusion.
- **Vice:** Envy. A Type 4 can easily become jealous of something that another person has since they are always searching for the missing pieces of their life.
- **Common Temptation:** Daydreaming. A Type 4 has to go to great efforts to remain grounded.
- **Common Desire:** To be themselves without any justification or reasoning.
- **Common Fear:** Losing their identity or purpose.
- **Exalted Ideals:** Genesis. A Type 4 can peel back the curtains of mystery and see how a series of events began. They can think backward, which helps

when they are trying to understand themselves.
- **Egoic Challenge:** Overindulgence in fantasy. Again, they have to go to great efforts to remain grounded here on earth.
- **Integration Point:** 1
- **Disintegration Point:** 2

Type 5: The Investigator and Observer

These are the quiet types of people. They would rather practice silence to absorb as much information as they can. Type 5s feel a longing to shatter ignorance and understand exactly how the world around them works. Acquisition of knowledge and seeing things in the bigger picture is what they aim to do. They are usually private people and will defend their independence fiercely. They can be frugal and may not share their resources. They can also be visionaries though and are able to root themselves in the present moment. They have an acute ability to maintain focus. They are capable of detaching themselves from circumstance and remain balanced in thought.

Type 5s can also be recognized as being arrogant or too guarded by other people. They may take the defensive more than the offensive and walk around with a shield that prevents others from getting close to them. By striving to do everything on their own, they can sometimes intimidate or offend people without trying to. They may also act as minimalists. They do not need many material possessions, but those that they do have, they cherish very deeply.

They are good problem solvers and can extrapolate complexities down into more manageable forms. Often, a Type 5 is thought of as someone deep and insightful. They also can come up with inventive ideas and find solutions to problems that stymie other people.

Their curious and probing nature can seem to lack emotions, and some people may view Type 5s more as robots than humans. Many of them are intellectuals which can either be a blessing or a curse when trying to bond with others.

These are the most natural loners. They do not do it to look cool either. They genuinely like spending time alone and not being hassled by other people's issues. Privacy and security are very important to type them. Don't expect them to rearrange their plans to make someone else feel good. A Type 5 may adopt the mindset of living without a want instead of pursuing it if it takes up too much of their time. If someone wants to get to know a Type 5, then they will have to present something of interest to them. Otherwise, the Type 5 will continue to study whatever they are already engaged in.

    Mentally, Type 5s have a natural ability to compartmentalize information. They can separate one thing from another instead of being bogged down by too many overlapping correspondences. This ability helps with their constant gathering of new information. They are also more left-brained, as in they think with the heads instead of their hearts. Emotions are another form of intellect to a Type 5, and they would rather think something through than feel it out. This can explode in the face of a Type 5 when they need an emotional outlet and do not look for one. They can become emotionally drained without realizing it and suffer negative consequences.

A Type 5 needs to let go of control. They know that they cannot control everything but may still try to do so anyway, creating a form of cognitive dissonance. They can also come across as rigid, guarded, and cold to other people. They can seem brutally arrogant and snobbish. They also do not give second chances very often. These traits can make bonding with a Type 5 very taxing, and people will give up on them. In turn, Type 5s give up on others just as easily.

Type 5s can have trouble feeling content since they think there is always more to learn. Even when they are content, they may mask it. They can also be a bit hard to follow and understand since they often refuse to see things from another – lesser – person's point of view. They can be mistaken for being greedy as well. Their loner nature makes establishing relationships very difficult. They can also place too much importance on their mind and ignore other aspects of life such as their reputations.

Spiritually speaking, a type 5 can use their focus and intellect to rise onto higher plains. They are also good at removing distractions and can use that to their advantage by placing spiritual work before everything else. Or, they can get too caught up in their intellect and forget to balance out the other aspects of themselves, thus, preventing them from acceding onto a higher sphere. They can struggle to find the medium between living for themselves and living for others.

Type 5 at a glance

- **Virtue:** Letting go. Type 5s can forget the past and move into the future.
- **Vice:** Grudge. This can act as the opposite of letting go. They can hoard onto the past and get trapped in the present, never being able to step into the future.
- **Common Temptation:** Misinterpretations. The tendency of a Type 5 to think in the bigger picture all the time can prevent them from noticing the importance of smaller details.
- **Common Desire:** To understand everything around them.
- **Common Fear:** Remaining in ignorance.

- **Exalted Ideals:** Human omniscience. They do not know all, but they can connect the dots so well that they may come across almost as psychic.
- **Egoic Challenge:** Not giving. Type 5s have to overcome their loner nature and let other people in, as well as share their wisdom and resources.
- **Integration Point:** 8
- **Disintegration Point:** 7

Type 6: The Loyalist and Skeptic

Type 6s swing on both ends of polarity. They can be the most excessive of worriers or the most trusting of all the dominant personality types. The main drives in their lives revolve around being safe and secure. They want to trust the world around them, but to be on the safe side, they will opt for preparation more than faith. They can share their trust openly or become showered by fear and clam up in a shell. It really can go either way. A Type 6 may walk around all day trying to balance both their trust and skepticism. They often won't let their guard down even though they long to.

Their devotion makes them some of the best team players that anyone will ever meet. Unless a type 6 becomes fearful, they will only bring benefits to whatever team they join. They have a high moral code and will defend other people and do what they can to uphold what they consider to be just. It may not be apparent when first meeting a 6, but they are very courageous. They have to be since fear is always trying to creep up on them. They do not abstain from commitments either. When a 6 makes a pledge, they will see it through. They are often prepared for the rougher patches of life as well. Type 6s are survivors.

Remember though, that there are many different versions of each personality type. A type 6 on the lower polarity can become obsessed with their fears. They are susceptible to phobias and paranoia. Anxiety can get the best of them. They are prone to bouts of confusion and may lack direction. Or, they may charge directly into their fears and deftly conquer them. Typically, a Type 6 will bounce from one extreme to the other. Some days, they will be too rattled to get much of anything done. On other days, they will be a force of efficiency and victory. Either way, they are very responsible people.

A Type 6 will look into their environment for challenges and solutions. They can become very effective problem solvers if they do not let their fears get the best of them. However, they can also be wary of solving a lot of problems simply by not trusting the solutions they come up with.

6s like to have trust in authority. They look for people of authority in their relationships and hope that those who have authority will help keep them safe. They always keep in mind though that those with authority can betray them, so this creates a wayward relationship often. Type 6s are known to ask a lot of questions of both friends and strangers alike. The more information they have, the more they can prepare themselves to remain safe.

The most important thing for a 6 to do is not focus on their fears. If their fears get out of hand, they can project them onto other people. When focusing on the positive, they are capable of bonding with almost anyone, but doing so is a constant challenge for them. They have to be careful not to drive people away by expressing too much fear. They are very in tune with their emotions and usually can detect the root cause of how they are feeling.

When functioning on a lower polarity, they can come across as a pessimist. Their attention to trust can also have a reverse effect.

People may become suspicious of them, and in turn, not trust them. 6s also tend to look too far into the future and worry about things that may never happen.

When a 6 is on a spiritual path, they must remember to maintain balance. Loyalty is a form of faith. Skepticism is a form of fear. Being either on one end or the other can lead them astray. They must find a middle ground and hold onto it if they are to rise to a higher plane of understanding.

Type 6 at a glance

- **Virtue:** Courage. A Type 6 can face their fears and crush them.
- **Vice:** Fear. If they do not face their fears, then they will be in a constant state of questioning everything.

- **Common Temptation:** Not making a choice. A Type 6 may choose inaction and not accomplish much of anything.
- **Common Desire:** To be given a clear roadmap of what to do. They would rather have others make decisions for them.
- **Common Fear:** Not having a roadmap and being left to figure out everything for themselves.
- **Exalted Ideals:** Absolute faith. This can lead them to overcome anything.
- **Egoic Challenge:** They need to focus on the positive instead of the negative.
- **Integration Point:** 9
- **Disintegration Point:** 3

Type 7: The Enthusiast

7s long to get the most that they can out of life. These are optimistic people and like to focus on the positive side of life. They enjoy play and can be thrill seekers. They can be either relaxed and pleasant or impulsive and easily distracted.

They require freedom, so they don't miss out on the opportunities that life can offer them. This makes them rather flexible and adventurous. They often like to look ahead at what tomorrow may bring. They can also become very focused and practical when trying to make sure that the future they envision will become reality.

A 7 can have trouble slowing down their mind. When introduced to a stimulus, they may have trouble ignoring it. This leads to rapid thoughts that may help or hurt them. Limitations do not sit well with 7s. When given the freedom to learn as they go, they excel in whatever they are doing.

7s are strong starters but poor finishers. Many jobs they start will never be finished. They will move onto the next thing before finishing the last. This is because they get bored very easily and need constant stimulation. Some of them can come across as adrenaline junkies and may be too wild for some people's taste. They can also be fidgety and jump from one topic to another before coming to any concrete conclusions. They are not the most patient people and have to be aware go to great lengths to not become restless.

These people are the life of the party and attention seekers. To some, this can come across as a flaw while others will view 7's as a source of raw energy. They can be hyper and have trouble calming down even in formal situations. They can also be escapist, and instead of solving their problems, they will just avoid them. They can also rewrite history in their minds and turn a negative experience into a positive one, which will delay them learning lessons properly. They do not handle well being told what to do or not do and can be prone to fights. However, they also tend to try and use humor to soften any negative vibes.

They tend to avoid facing their fears which can stunt their growth. They do not realize that always having a positive mindset in itself is limiting. They are also poor listeners since their minds are always racing a mile a minute. They tend to avoid looking at themselves and instead, blame other people for other things that have gone wrong.

When a 7 is on a spiritual path, they must remember to calm down. There is a proper time to use all their energy, but it can also lead them to believe in things that simply are not true. If a 7 can learn to direct their energy correctly, then they can open up astral gates that were previously closed. If they don't learn how to control their energy, they will only delude themselves into thinking they have reached a higher plane of being, when in reality, they have only been running in circles.

Type 7 at a glance

- **Virtue:** Sobriety. A typical 7 does not need any substance to make life more interesting for them.

- **Vice:** Overindulgence. When not controlled, their affirming nature can get out of hand and lead to excess.
- **Common Temptation:** Always looking outward for the next thrill. They should look more within to find completion.
- **Common Desire:** To feel fulfilled.
- **Common Fear:** Not having freedom.
- **Exalted Ideals:** Pain and wisdom. If a 7 can focus their energy on both understanding the positive and negative, they can literally accomplish anything.
- **Egoic Challenge:** Always anticipating what comes next. 7s need to practice living in the moment instead of looking for the next dose of excitement.
- **Integration Point:** 5
- **Disintegration Point:** 1

Type 8: The Challenger and Protector

Out of all the personality types, this one needs to let go of the need to control more than any other. Having control makes 8s feel as if they have value. They are not comfortable showing vulnerability. These are very strong people, but even the strong have weaknesses. Type 8s need to come to terms with that.

They look forward to challenges and will deftly defend what they value, people or otherwise. Most 8s are personable because they are so strong, others like to be around them and feel the field of their protection. Or, they can be too forceful and may try to overpower others. They often try to appear larger than life, and by doing so can become intimidating. They can also confuse their own sense of worth by thinking they are the most important people on the planet.

They do not depend on other people and rather try to get others to depend upon them. They can be aggressive and quick to action, even hasty at times. When they make a decision, they stick to it, even if it was the wrong choice. They are fighters, and they want everyone to know and respect it.

They like to be the cause, not the effect and can toss influence onto others. Intense and direct are two words that can sum up a Type 8. A common mistake that 8s make is by labeling other people as strong or weak without taking the entire human into consideration. Again, they can be hasty and do not like to admit when they are wrong. They can also view the world either as black or white and are not the best at blending different elements together.

An easy way to offend an 8 is to ignore them. They are larger than life, and by ignoring them, a knife is stabbed into their pride. Another thing that bothers them is giving them a task to do that is beneath them. When 8's are not in charge, they are more likely to rebel then protect. They are also not the best at exploring their emotions. Many human emotions reveal weakness, and 8s are weak to weakness. They may not realize this, but by not admitting their flaws, they are only highlighting those same flaws. They can also easily ruin a good situation by not compromising. Not compromising is also a weakness. They like to make up their own rules and can become rebellious for no good reason. They may also step forward to be a leader when they are not the best suited for the job. When an 8 is in control and everyone is subservient to them, there is no trouble. When they lose control, they can be hellish. Yet, 8s will defend those they care for to the death. They will fight until the battle is won.

Spiritually, an 8 can be comparable to the zodiac sign of Leo. They are a fiery lion, fixed fire. If they can direct their power, and let go of the need for power, they can ascend as high as they want. If they can't control their power and let go, they will keep on fighting the same fight against themselves until the day they die. Another word that should be attributed to the 8s is *passion*. The 8s will either be enslaved by their passions and fall victim to them, or they will win the fight against their passions and use that energy to better themselves. If an 8 can control their passions, then they cannot just reach a higher plane of being but storm the gates of heaven with the raw power of a flaming red lion.

Type 8 at a glance

Virtue: Innocence. Aside from their characteristics, 8's really does not understand that they have flaws. They also don't grasp that they have anything to improve upon. However, if they have put in the work to improve themselves instead of ignoring their negative traits, then they truly are innocent. Innocent – as in free from error.

Vice: Lust. This is not just sexual, but they can be overly forceful.

Common Temptation: Believing they have no limits. At some point, this mindset will destroy them. They have to control their passions.

Common Desire: Not needing anyone else besides themselves.

Common Fear: Being defeated, bested, losing, not being able to protect themselves or others.

Exalted Ideals: Truth. Since they believe in themselves so much, they don't have any reason to purposefully lie, although they lie to themselves often without realizing it.

Egoic Challenge: Vengeance. Again, 8s need to learn to let go and stop the fight.

Integration Point: 2

Disintegration Point: 5

Type 9: The Peacemaker and Mediator

People of this type are in a constant search for harmony, not just for themselves but also for the rest of the world. Peace, stability, and balance are few words used to describe Type 9s. Type 9s will go far out of their way to avoid conflict. These people would rather choose to avoid arguments even if doing so besmirches their reputations. On a lower polarity, they may act as procrastinators.

When viewing the word *mediator* of the Type 9 personality, don't think of it so much as a negotiation between two people, but linking the peace of nature with themselves. Such a statement may sound abstract, but Type 9s are cut from a different cloth. They seek to be at one with the world and universe.

The emotions and actions of other people can greatly affect Type 9s. They do not have a high tolerance against others who are in bad moods and will often try to lift their spirits, or just ignore them. They are fantastic listeners and are able to see any situation from several different points of view. They are patient and very supportive of other people.

9s have an innate ability to let go and move on. Because of this, they seem to have a great impact on the environment around them. 9s often choose not to disturb the peace around them which can present them as pacifists to other people. They can also be a predictable group and often choose daily patterns that help keep them at ease. They live to avoid conflict and stress.

9s would rather form tight bonds with people than have a superficial relationship. They often feel very intense emotions but are capable of maintaining them and remaining even-tempered. This can mask the truth of how a 9 is really feeling as they may choose to not project their true feelings onto others, leaving people wondering what they are really thinking.

9s can be stubborn. They may be so averse to conflict that they simply let unjust actions happen without doing anything to stop them. In their pursuit of being in harmony with everyone, they can keep too much of an open mind at times and may let wickedness go unchallenged. They can show the darker side of mercy, as in being merciful to those who are wicked and by proxy, spreading more wickedness. They may also try to remain calm when they are really not, and by doing so, they wind up masking their true selves which will keep them out of balance with those they are trying to bond with. They cannot also recognize some of their more negative aspects and take a very long time to improve their weaknesses.

They do not manage anger well. Being angry to a 9 can sap all of their energy, and then they will suffer a long spell of lethargy. It can take them a very long time to recover from an argument or bout of anger. In fact, they may not even notice that they are upset and avoid the conflict going on within themselves. This causes them to not develop the proper coping skills to deal with anger, and they never get any better at managing it. This is one of their biggest challenges to remaining at peace.

The ironic thing about a 9 is that they are not easy to manipulate. Since they can let go so easily, they can just walk away. This can confound the people that are trying to influence them. By letting go, the 9 has gained more control. A 9 may also, when they finally do express their opinion, be long-winded in their explanations. This can make them a bore to many other people and difficult to communicate with.

9s often display passive aggressive behavior without realizing it. This can be a damaging blow to their reputations. Type 9s are often the targets of gossip but will not do anything to stop it. They will simply accept it and carry on.

Spiritually, Type 9s are proponents of meditation. They are the calm waters. The only major downside to this is leaving wickedness unchecked. A type 9 may be able to raise their consciousness, but when they re-enter the world of other people, they will have a hard time maintaining their peace. So, they will walk away again, let go, and repeat the pattern all over. If anything, they need to be a bit more assertive and not shy away from conflict. If a type 9 were to seek their highest virtues, which involve proper discernment of consequences for their actions, they very well may be able to ascend past the normal boundary of human perception. Of course, such a platitude would take much training, but they aim to be at total peace with nature and accomplishing such a feat will not come quickly no matter what techniques they use.

    9 is a number of completions, the last digit before a new cycle begins again. If someone with the dominant personality of a 9 were to put in the work and understand that there may come a time when they will have to end their passivity and step into action, then a whole new world of wisdom may just be found resting at their feet. If they find that new wisdom and understand it, then they can reenter the world of other people and be able to

maintain their sense of peace better than before.

Type 9 at a glance

- **Virtue:** Action orientated. This does not mean that Type 9s jump into action, but that they are able to discern between which actions will have bad consequences. This is a major reason why they often choose to not act and maintain passive.
- **Vice:** Laziness. When a 9 is not operating at their best, they may take inaction too far and not do much of anything.
- **Common Temptation:** To avoid stress, conflict, and not take chances or stir the pot.

- **Common Desire:** To have peace of mind – no more problems.
- **Common Fear:** Being out of balance with themselves.
- **Exalted Ideals:** Love. Don't think of love in terms of romance, but more so as the two things being attracted and joined together. They seek the love of nature.
- **Egoic Challenge:** 9s have to try hard to remain down to earth and remember that life is a balance between the positive and the negative. They must keep in mind that one cannot exist without the other.
- **Integration Point:** 3
- **Disintegration Point:** 6

Chapter 5: The Wings

The Wings are the secondary personality traits. These are the less apparent pieces of the human psyche that mix in with the dominant personality. Your secondary personality traits can not only add to the pool of the self, but it can sometimes be in direct opposition to a dominant personality. This concept is often overlooked.

To fully understand the self, every aspect (no matter how small) of the personality must be observed. Take a look at the image of the Enneagram again. As you know, there are 9 dominant types of personalities. To explain the Wings, we will use number 9 (The Peacemaker and Mediator) as an example. 9 is between 1, and 8. 1 and 8 are the Wings of someone who has a Type 9 personality.

Yes, it's that simple. Whatever your dominant personality number is, the numbers to its right and left are its wings. Someone who is a 9 will have all of the characteristics of either a 1 or an 8, a perfectionist or a challenger. These will always be secondary to the dominant personality traits, but they are still always active at the same time. So not only do you have to learn everything you can about your dominant personality to truly know yourself, but you must also learn the proponents of your Wing as well. Maybe it is not so simple. Self-discovery is a lifelong process, and the journey will not end until the life does.

Some people only have one wing, while others have two. Figuring out what your Wing is can be very tricky, and if you are unsure whether you have one or two, then the road to illumination can become even more confusing. The best advice that can be given to assist with this is to figure out what your dominant personality is, and then look at both of the possible Wings. If one of the descriptions for a Wing resonates with you more than another, begin focusing on that. If both of the Wings resonate, select one to focus on first and learn as much about it as you can before moving onto the next one. Don't attempt to discover or alter too much about yourself all at once. There may be a temptation to do so, but it is better to work slowly with the Enneagram in the beginning.

It should be made clear that just knowing your dominant personality type and its Wing will not give you the full spectrum of the personality. There are also the integration/disintegration points and different levels of health-related to how someone's personality expresses itself. Due to so many different factors being involved, two separate people who are both Type 3 (or any other number) may behave quite differently. To fully understand your own personality, remember this formula. Write it down next to the diagram of the Enneagram you were told to draw earlier in this book.

Dominant Personality + Wing(s) + Integration point + Disintegration point + Health Level of Personality = TRUE SELF

To clarify, let's use personality type 3 as an example. 3 is between the numbers 2 and 4. For this example, we will assume that 2 is the Wing. We will also assume that the current level of health for this example is a 5. We know that the integration point for a 3 is 6 and the disintegration point is 9.

Dominant Personality **(3)** + Wing(s) **(2)** + Integration point **(3)** + Disintegration point **(6)** + Health Level of Personality **(5)** = TRUE SELF **(3, 2, 3, 6, 5)**

Many people have wrongly tried to promote the Enneagram as a fast track to self-discovery. This is not how the Enneagram was meant to be used. The Enneagram is meant to be studied and meditated upon time and time again. The Enneagram is meant to be fully understood that someone can use it to summon up different personas and become the type of person they need to be for whatever challenge they have to face.

Think of it like this; you live inside the Enneagram as your dominant personality with both its positive and negative traits. As you move through life inside the Enneagram, you learn how to shed your dominant personality when coming across a challenge that it cannot overcome and adopt one of the other personality types to defeat the challenge your dominant personality lacked the tools to deal with. Later, you will always return to your dominant personality as that is your main house. To do this would make you a master of the Enneagram, and thus, a master of life.

Chapter 6: Health of the Self

When two different people both have the same dominant personality type, they may still behave quite differently. This is not just because of the Wings, but also the level of health (or development) that someone's personality is currently at. If two Type 1s are at different levels of health, then the characteristics of their dominant personality will not manifest exactly the same. Someone who is healthier than someone else of the same type or at a higher stage of development will be able to control their negative traits easier.

For example, one of the negative traits of a Type 8 is that they can be domineering and intimidating. If a Type 8 is currently at an average stage of health, then they will probably fluctuate back and forth between controlling their domineering nature and being controlled by it. If they are healthier, above the average range, then they will be able to control their domineering nature better and only use it when needed. If they are lower than the average range, they will have no control and will constantly be projecting their forcefulness on everyone around them. However, a positive aspect of a Type 8 is that they can protect what they care about. If they are in the average range of health, then they will be able to correctly pick and choose who and what they want to protect. If they are above the average range of health, then they will not only be able to protect what they care about but be able to use the right amount of force – and select the correct strategy – when playing the role of a defender. If they are below the average range of health, then they won't so much protect something but simply become a rebel without a cause and argue just to argue without protecting anything in the process.

This is an extremely important part of studying the Enneagram because it is one of the explanations for why and how someone's personality can change with time. None of the levels of heath are locked in place. During one single day, someone may move about the scale of health rapidly depending on the amounts of stress and good luck they are encountering. To truly know yourself though, you still have to pinpoint where your personalities' current level of health is.

There are 9 different levels of health which are all grouped into three separate sets. We will start at the bottom, the unhealthiest level, and work our way to the top.

Unhealthy Levels

Level 9: Self-Destruction – At this stage, the person does not have any control over their personality. They are nothing more than a walking ego that reacts to the world around them. They are like a deer that runs away when scared or a dog that bites the hand that feeds it out of impulse or confusion. They don't think, only act. They don't build themselves up, only destroy. They have absolutely no control over themselves. Spiritually speaking, this is the stage of Hell.

Level 8: Obsessive Compulsion – At this level, someone does maintain some control over their actions, but only to a small degree. Subconscious habits dictate the person's patterns and activities. There is often a cycle of repetition at this stage. The body will do several small tasks without the self-conscious realizing it. These behaviors may not be self-destructive but can fall into that category if not managed properly.

Level 7: Violation – This is when the person is beginning to cause harm to themselves. They have awareness that they lack self-control but can't do much to counteract it. They are violating their own will. They know something is wrong and want improvement but continue to defy themselves. Many people with addictions they want to quit are operating at this level. In other areas of their lives, they may actually have self-control, but every time they give into the addiction again, they drop down to this level, if only for a short time.

Average Levels

Level 6: Overcompensation – One level below self-control. The mind will recognize that there is a lack of willpower, and instead of working directly on the trouble areas, the subconscious will exaggerate the qualities that the self-conscious does have control over. Compare it to the basketball player that can't shoot a free-throw but can perform a slam dunk. Instead of improving their free-throw, they will constantly go for more slam dunks.

Level 5: Self-Control – This is the medium level that most people operate on. When you wake up in the morning, you are probably working at this stage. There is self-control, but it can be altered depending on what else happens through the course of the day.

Level 4: Social Control – People at this stage can maintain their self-control even when the environment around them is trying to influence them. They are not swayed, for better or worse, by peer pressure or social conventions. They remain true to themselves even while the world is fluctuating around them.

__Healthy Levels__

Level 3: Social Understanding – This is when someone truly knows their place and value in the world. They fully grasp the effect they have on others as well as the effect others have on them. People at this stage are not swayed by stimulus or moral conventions. No matter what is going on or where they are, they remain in control of themselves.

Level 2: Psychological Understanding – Many would describe this stage as the highest point a person can reach. This is a true and complete understanding of who you are. You recognize your vices, virtues, and can alter both of them at any given time no matter where you are or what is going on. Even when someone changes their personality to a different level, people who have been at this stage can recognize the change and manage things properly. When people reach the second level, they can control their desires, alter their personality as they need to, and move about the Enneagram as they want. They can trace every thought and emotion back to its source and stop those emotions from escalating.

Level 1: Self Freedom – Most people never reach or can even fathom this stage. This is the level of absolute control. The personality can be completely altered by the person at their command. All impulses and urges are switches that the person can turn on or off as they see fit. There are no desires or questions. The person is at total peace with who they are. Spiritually speaking, this is complete unity with God. According to some authorities on the Enneagram, this stage is beyond human comprehension.

Integration and Disintegration Points

The above-mentioned levels of health are in regard to how the entire personality changes as a whole. The integration and disintegration points only relate to how the dominant personality changes.

When a stressful stimulus interacts with someone, the stress will cause their personality to drop or disintegrate into another type of personality. Opposite of that, when someone receives good fortune, their personality will grow or integrate into another type of personality. When feeling good or bad, a different dominant personality type will take over temporarily. If someone has a Type 1 dominant personality functioning at a level 6 of health, and they become stressed, they will behave like a Type 4 functioning at a level 6 of health. If that same person, a Type 1 functioning at a level 6 of health, receives good fortune, then they will behave like a Type 7 functioning at a level 6 of health. They will always return to their dominant personality type afterward, and the integration/disintegration points do not affect the overall level of health that they are currently functioning on.

The mind needs a way to deal with stress and luck. Temporarily moving from one personality type to another, but always having a dominant type to return to, is nature's way of letting people segment different aspects of themselves. This is why it is important to remember that there is no superior personality. The levels of health are the only piece of the personality that can be considered superior or inferior. With proper knowledge about the self and effort, the levels of health can be altered since none of them are set in stone. The integration/disintegration points are just another part of who you really are.

Integration Points

When someone receives a boost to their mood, they will temporarily switch from their normal dominant personality to another dominant personality. The flow of integration is as follows;

- A Type 1 will behave as a Type 7.
- A Type 2 will behave as a Type 4.
- A Type 3 will behave as a Type 6.
- A Type 4 will behave as a Type 1.
- A Type 5 will behave as a Type 8.
- A Type 6 will behave as a Type 9.
- A Type 7 will behave as a Type 1.
- A Type 8 will behave as a Type 2.
- A Type 9 will behave as a Type 3.

Disintegration Points

When someone becomes stressed, they will temporarily switch from their normal dominant personality to another dominant personality. The flow of disintegration is as follows;

- A Type 1 will behave as a Type 4.
- A Type 2 will behave as a Type 8.
- A Type 3 will behave as a Type 9.
- A Type 4 will behave as a Type 2.
- A Type 5 will behave as a Type 7.
- A Type 6 will behave as a Type 3.
- A Type 7 will behave as a Type 1.
- A Type 8 will behave as a Type 5.
- A Type 9 will behave as a Type 6.

Now that you have been fully introduced to the Enneagram, this formula is worth repeating.

Dominant Personality + Wing(s) + Integration point + Disintegration point + Health Level of Personality = TRUE SELF

Chapter 7: Personality Test

Please bear in mind that general personality tests may not resonate with everyone or be entirely accurate. If you expect a quick test to tell you everything about who you really are, you have been misled by charlatans and fads. Consider this personality test a start to self-discovery and only a start, nothing more. This should give you a basic starting point to figure out your dominant personality type. For the level of health regarding your personality, you will have to determine that yourself (but remember that it can fluctuate). For the integration/disintegration points, check the earlier references listed in this book.

Get a pen and piece of paper. Write down your answers to these questions. Every time you answer YES, write down the number 1 for your answer. Every time you answer NO, write down the number 2. Every time you answer SOMEWHAT, write down the number 3. Every time you answer UNSURE, write down the number 4. Different parts of the test are allotted to different types of dominant personality types. At the end, you will tally up your score for each section. There are 10 questions to each part. The minimal score for each part is 10. The maximum is 40. What is most important about this test is not the overall score. What you need to pay attention to is what area you have scored lowest or highest in.

PART 1

I begin planning my next project before the current one is completed.

YES NO SOMEWHAT UNSURE

I have everything I want in my life.

YES NO SOMEWHAT UNSURE

I would rather stay at home on my day off than go out.

YES   NO   SOMEWHAT   UNSURE

I like to stay awake all night.

YES   NO   SOMEWHAT   UNSURE

I am a morning person.

YES   NO   SOMEWHAT   UNSURE

I think there is life after death.

YES   NO   SOMEWHAT   UNSURE

New people frighten me.

YES   NO   SOMEWHAT   UNSURE

I only like to be with other people who share my interests.

YES   NO   SOMEWHAT   UNSURE

I think therapy is for the weak.

YES   NO   SOMEWHAT   UNSURE

I would rather work alone than with other people.

YES   NO   SOMEWHAT   UNSURE

PART 2

I do not like receiving negative feedback.

YES   NO   SOMEWHAT   UNSURE

The world is unfair.

YES   NO   SOMEWHAT   UNSURE

I am very critical towards both myself and others.

YES   NO   SOMEWHAT   UNSURE

I want to be recognized as being successful.

YES   NO   SOMEWHAT   UNSURE

I never become depressed.

YES   NO   SOMEWHAT   UNSURE

I give strangers the benefit of the doubt.

YES   NO   SOMEWHAT   UNSURE

I want people to trust me.

YES   NO   SOMEWHAT   UNSURE

I try to get people with authority to consider me as an equal.

YES   NO   SOMEWHAT   UNSURE

When stressed, I do not make decisions.

YES   NO   SOMEWHAT   UNSURE

I enjoy helping others.

YES   NO   SOMEWHAT   UNSURE

PART 3

People admire me, and I like it.

YES   NO   SOMEWHAT   UNSURE

I can easily calm my emotions.

YES   NO   SOMEWHAT   UNSURE

I do not like expressing my emotions to other people.

YES   NO   SOMEWHAT   UNSURE

When bothered by negativity, I can distract myself with other activities.

YES   NO   SOMEWHAT   UNSURE

I lack ambition.

YES   NO   SOMEWHAT   UNSURE

I easily recognize errors.

YES   NO   SOMEWHAT   UNSURE

I take more then I give.

YES NO SOMEWHAT UNSURE

I am suspicious even towards people I know well.

YES NO SOMEWHAT UNSURE

I am dominant over other people.

YES NO SOMEWHAT UNSURE

I don't care about other people's problems.

YES NO SOMEWHAT UNSURE

PART 4

I am very organized.

YES NO SOMEWHAT UNSURE

Romance is very important to me.
YES NO SOMEWHAT UNSURE

I do not judge other people.
YES NO SOMEWHAT UNSURE

I often compare myself to others.
YES NO SOMEWHAT UNSURE

Close relationship matters more to me than anything else.
YES NO SOMEWHAT UNSURE

I often wonder if I am the center of gossip.
YES NO SOMEWHAT UNSURE

I am a risk taker.

YES   NO   SOMEWHAT   UNSURE

I am intimidating to others.

YES   NO   SOMEWHAT   UNSURE

I am genuine with other people.

YES   NO   SOMEWHAT   UNSURE

I detest slackers.

YES   NO   SOMEWHAT   UNSURE

PART 5

I hate being interrupted.

YES   NO   SOMEWHAT   UNSURE

I avoid making commitments.
YES   NO   SOMEWHAT   UNSURE

I readily impress people.
YES   NO   SOMEWHAT   UNSURE

I do what others want without resistance.
YES   NO   SOMEWHAT.   UNSURE

I place safety first at all times.
YES   NO   SOMEWHAT   UNSURE

Mood swings are common to me.

YES   NO   SOMEWHAT   UNSURE

I like to explore intense emotions.
YES   NO   SOMEWHAT   UNSURE

I long to fit in with a group.
YES   NO   SOMEWHAT   UNSURE

I am very detail-orientated.
YES   NO   SOMEWHAT   UNSURE

My decisions are based on how much fun I think I will have.
YES   NO   SOMEWHAT   UNSURE

PART 6

I am a loner, but do not want to be.
YES   NO   SOMEWHAT   UNSURE

I would rather be alone than around other people.
YES   NO   SOMEWHAT   UNSURE

I will help others before I help myself.
YES   NO   SOMEWHAT   UNSURE

I do not handle confrontation well.
YES   NO   SOMEWHAT   UNSURE

I thrive during competition.
YES   NO   SOMEWHAT   UNSURE

I am congenial towards everyone I meet.

YES   NO   SOMEWHAT   UNSURE

Being considered a failure is my greatest fear.

YES   NO   SOMEWHAT   UNSURE

I am selfish and proud of it.

YES   NO   SOMEWHAT   UNSURE

I have trouble saving money.

YES   NO   SOMEWHAT   UNSURE

I think that a fight can bring people closer together.

YES   NO   SOMEWHAT   UNSURE

PART 7

I believe there is a good quality to being sad.

YES   NO   SOMEWHAT   UNSURE

I have lots of energy.

YES   NO   SOMEWHAT   UNSURE

I can control my temper.

YES   NO   SOMEWHAT   UNSURE

I never back down from a challenge.

YES   NO   SOMEWHAT   UNSURE

I am slow to start new things.
YES   NO   SOMEWHAT   UNSURE

I will continue to work until the job is done.
YES   NO   SOMEWHAT   UNSURE

I always see the silver lining.
YES   NO   SOMEWHAT   UNSURE

I look for things that are wrong more than things that are right.
YES   NO   SOMEWHAT   UNSURE

Having a spotlight on me makes me anxious.
YES   NO   SOMEWHAT   UNSURE

I lack confidence.

YES NO   SOMEWHAT UNSURE

PART 8

I look for the good in people instead of the bad.

YES NO   SOMEWHAT UNSURE

I avoid change at all cost.

YES NO   SOMEWHAT UNSURE

I am more unique than most people.

YES NO   SOMEWHAT UNSURE

I don't ever need help.

YES NO   SOMEWHAT UNSURE

I am tough as nails.

YES   NO   SOMEWHAT UNSURE

Other people are left wondering what I am really thinking.

YES   NO   SOMEWHAT UNSURE

I am too modest.

YES   NO   SOMEWHAT UNSURE

I have trouble keeping focus.

YES   NO   SOMEWHAT UNSURE

I am very disciplined.

YES   NO   SOMEWHAT UNSURE

I can be dramatic.

YES   NO   SOMEWHAT   UNSURE

PART 9

I second guess myself.

YES   NO   SOMEWHAT   UNSURE

I enjoy fantasy more than reality.

YES   NO   SOMEWHAT   UNSURE

I do not make decisions quickly.

YES   NO   SOMEWHAT   UNSURE

I become bored easily.

YES   NO   SOMEWHAT   UNSURE

I think most people are liars.
YES   NO   SOMEWHAT   UNSURE

I often genuflect.
YES   NO   SOMEWHAT   UNSURE

I fall asleep easily.
YES   NO   SOMEWHAT   UNSURE

I am the life of the party.
YES   NO   SOMEWHAT.   UNSURE

I think of the past often.
YES   NO   SOMEWHAT   UNSURE

I have a vivid imagination.

YES   NO   SOMEWHAT   UNSURE

PART 10

There is always something to be thankful for.

YES   NO   SOMEWHAT   UNSURE

I give people second chances.

YES   NO   SOMEWHAT   UNSURE

If I die tomorrow, I would have no regrets.

YES   NO   SOMEWHAT   UNSURE

When one chapter ends, another will always begin.

YES   NO   SOMEWHAT UNSURE

I think I am smarter than most people.
YES   NO   SOMEWHAT UNSURE

I enjoy the great outdoors.
YES   NO   SOMEWHAT UNSURE

I am careful about what I eat.
YES   NO   SOMEWHAT UNSURE

I would rather spend time with family more than anyone else.
YES NO SOMEWHAT. UNSURE

I do not like my family.
YES   NO   SOMEWHAT UNSURE

I often have high expectations.
YES   NO   SOMEWHAT   UNSURE

ANSWER KEY

If you scored highest in parts 1 or 2, you are probably a Type 1.

If you scored highest in parts 2 or 3, you are probably a Type 2.

If you scored highest in parts 3 or 4, you are probably a Type 3.

If you scored highest in parts 4 or 5, you are probably a Type 4.

If you scored highest in parts 5 or 6, you are probably a Type 5.

If you scored highest in parts 6 or 7, you are probably a Type 6.

If you scored highest in parts 7 or 8, you are probably a Type 7.

If you scored highest in parts 8 or 9, you are probably a Type 8.

If you scored highest in parts 9 or 10, you are probably a Type 9.

These groupings may require some explanation. Let's say you scored highest in section 2. That means you are either a Type 2 or Type 3. Or, if you scored highest in section 4, you are either a Type 3 or 4. A Wing of Type 2 is 3, and a Wing of Type 3 is 2. The other Wing of Type 3 is 4. The Wings of 4 are 3 and 5. This pattern continues throughout the rest of the answer key. This test was designed to take the Wings into account, without being able to directly interact with the test taker (you). That is why the word "either" is listed in the Answer Key. If you scored highest in sections 2, then you can determine that you are probably a Type 2 with a Wing of 3. If you scored highest in section 4, then you can determine that you are probably a Type 4 with a wing of 3. If you scored highest in section 10, then you are probably a Type 9 with a Wing of 1. Yet you could be a Type 9 with a wing of 8. This test may not be entirely conclusive, but again, none really are no matter what anyone tries to tell you. It is a starting point though to lead you in the direction you need to go so you can begin to pinpoint your dominant personality type and wing and get to work discovering the rest of yourself after.

Determining exactly if you have the qualities of both Wings, or only one, can't be entirely concluded with just a simple test. You will have to review the chapter on the 9 different personality types again and look into which Type you believe to be your wing, or if you have more than one Wing.

If you have scored highest in more than one section of the test, then you may want to look at those sections again. Take more time to look over the questions and see if you answered them as truthful as possible. This is a common problem with general personality tests. When many people first try taking one, they often realize they don't know themselves well enough to give honest answers. No one is claiming that you have lied on purpose, but you may have made a mistake out of confusion – or some of these questions you may never have spent much time thinking about.

There are other personality tests out there in the world besides this one. The best thing you can do is take more than just one and see what your average is. If several tests, this one included, determine that you are a Type 6 (just as an example), then you can assume you are a Type 6 and continue your journey from there.

Practical Advice

Taking more than one tests is a good start. Simply putting in the effort to read this book was also a good start. Yet, the only way to really discover who you are is to take a chance and try out new things that you have not done before. Go and meet new people that you usually wouldn't interact with. Go visit a location that is outside of your normal haunts. Take up an activity that you have never done before. Expand your horizons, try new things, soak in new stimulus, and see how you react to them. If you meditate, start exercising, or try a different method of meditation than you have before. If you exercise, start meditating or try out a new form of exercise. If you watch TV, read a book instead. If you are an avid reader, watch some TV. The point is, do something new. If you don't ever try out new things, you will not be able to put your personality to the real test which is called LIFE and see the real practical results firsthand.

Oscar Ichazo seems to have faded away from the spotlight. Although he was the man that helped to reveal the Enneagram, his methods and instructions have fallen by the wayside. It is said that he created dance routines for his students and structured individual tasks and lessons for them to complete to discover their true personality. As Oscar Ichazo has stepped away from the spotlight, so have his techniques. They have been replaced by people who talk more than they do and make false guarantees. It has also been reported that Oscar Ichazo did not support what many people who came after he tried to do with the Enneagram – turn it into a scheme to make money by guaranteeing that self-discovery is right around the corner. Self-improvement takes work and exactly what kind of work is needed will be different on a case by case basis. The absolute best practical advice that can be given will not be found inside this book or any book. It can only be found inside of yourself. That is what the Enneagram was really constructed for in the first place – to give you a starting point for learning more about yourself. A starting point, not the final conclusion. Use the Enneagram to give you a peek behind the curtain that you have hidden from your true-self. After you have gotten a glimpse of who you really are, then you can slowly continue to pull out more and more of your own personal truth until the false personality accepts letting go and hands over the reins of truth to who you really are. If you can accomplish that, then the only thing left to do will be to walk the road of liberation.

    Best of luck.

Conclusion

Thank you for making it through to the end of *Enneagram*. Let's hope it was informative and able to provide you with all of the tools you need to achieve your goals whatever they may be.

The next step is to figure out what your dominant personality type is. Then you will have to determine what your Wing is. Make sure you take note of the integration and disintegration points for your dominant personality type. Then you can begin to figure out what level of health your personality is currently at. When you have discovered all of these integral pieces of the personality, you can start to bring them together to discover who you truly are. That is only the beginning of the journey of self-discovery though. If you truly want to know yourself down to the tiniest detail, then you must continue self-examination as you continue to grow older. Remember that the Enneagram is meant to be studied for an entire lifetime. It is an emblem and system of knowledge that will continue to emit enlightenment for as long as someone continues studying it. As you continue to change, the Enneagram will always be there to explain why you have changed, and what you have changed into. Be sure to continue using the Enneagram. Return to it whenever you are bogged down by confusion. It is a tool meant to become a master of yourself.